MONTECITO STYLE

MONTECITO STYLE

PARADISE ON CALIFORNIA'S GOLD COAST

PHOTOGRAPHS BY FIROOZ ZAHEDI
TEXT BY LORIE DEWHIRST PORTER
FOREWORD BY MARC APPLETON

M

CONTENTS

ABOUT FORTY YEARS AGO I was invited for a weekend at a home north of Los Angeles, somewhere near Santa Barbara, by a friend from college days and her husband, a well-known Hollywood actor. It was my first visit to that area. I drove up from LA and wondered about the houses and lifestyles shielded from view by the lush greenery that ran from the Santa Ynez mountains down to the Pacific Ocean. I didn't really know anything about the architecture of this part of California, but that evening, when I took the exit off the freeway and drove up toward the mountains, I could see grand mansions peeking out from behind their gates and hedges and was instantly transported back to the beautiful architecture along the Mediterranean coast, which I had frequented while growing up in Europe.

And the more I saw up close, the more I learned. My hosts' home was a classic example of a Spanish Colonial Revival mansion built in 1922. The hostess, a lady of impeccable taste, had decorated it in an elegant yet comfortable manner to complement the architecture. Tiered gardens stepped down the hill toward a magnificent swimming pool surrounded by Neoclassical urns and columns. It was a strong vision of California style—or one kind, at least.

I had arrived in Montecito. The feeling of that party in that setting never left me: the house, the gardens, the moon reflected in the swimming pool, the ocean, the fragrance of jasmine and rosemary in the soft air. On later visits I discovered that life in Montecito was not reserved just for the rich and famous. Whether middle class or among the Hollywood cadre who had second homes, everyone was there for the mild climate and peaceful environment between the

PREFACE
FIROOZ ZAHEDI

ocean and the mountains. The community was also a haven for people who respected each other's privacy, a major draw for the high-profile residents.

The more time I spent in Montecito and the more homes I visited, the more I learned about the architectural styles across different eras. There were the traditional mansions and newly built palazzi, but there were also cottages, low-slung midcentury modern houses, and even a major example of a brutalist house from the 1970s. Over time it became clear how the residents used their homes as showcases for their own creative expression, whether to display antiques sourced from around the world or showcase leading collections of contemporary art. In making this book, I wanted to represent its spectrum of interiors and gardens that span classical to contemporary, eclectic to eccentric—each in its own way defined by the particular taste and artistic vision of the owners.

Years after that first memorable moonlit party, my wife and I bought our own home here. Today Montecito is in the news as even more celebrities move in, yet it still offers much the same level of seclusion that had made it the hideaway of days gone by. I want to honor this special place through this book, expressing the aesthetic vision of homeowners who have created their own enchanting and enviable environments, reflecting the natural beauty around them in this lovely corner of California.

M ONTECITO (SPANISH FOR "LITTLE MOUNTAIN") is a small community of less than ten square miles within Santa Barbara County on the California coast. Since the late nineteenth century, it has enjoyed a reputation as an exclusive residential enclave that has resisted population growth and only reluctantly tolerated change in the face of progress. The widening of State Route 101, the highway that cuts through Montecito on its way from Los Angeles to San Francisco, has been accomplished everywhere else in its course through various communities over the decades, but it is only now underway in Montecito, the last remaining holdout—and only under duress of eminent domain.

The area's first residents were the Chumash people, who were ultimately subjugated by the Spanish. The Santa Barbara Mission, "The Queen of the Missions," established in 1786, was the tenth built by the Spanish in California in their quest to dominate the indigenous culture and convert the local population to Roman Catholicism. Spain's rule was finally overthrown in 1821 by newly independent Mexico, which in turn lost the

FOREWORD
MARC APPLETON

territory to the United States in 1848. The appeal of Santa Barbara as a California destination began with the gold rush and has continued ever since.

Although it generally faces west, the California coast gradually rotates southwest as it proceeds north from Los Angeles. Montecito and its adjacent communities actually face due south over the Pacific Ocean, disorienting most visitors and creating a geographic bearing not dissimilar to the Mediterranean coast in the South of France. The Santa Ynez range rises suddenly from the area's beaches, creating a backdrop and climate also comparable to Montecito's Mediterranean counterpart. Little wonder, then, that visitors who had traveled to Europe's Mediterranean countries were struck by the similarities.

In his *Transatlantic Sketches* (1875), Henry James observed of California that it seemed "a sort of prepared but unconscious Italy, the primitive *plate*, in perfect condition, but with the impression of History all yet to be made." What followed was indeed a new history for Southern California, and particularly Santa Barbara. Although wealthy Americans had traditionally headed to Europe on the Grand Tour in search of romantic Mediterranean destinations, their own country began offering attractive alternatives. With its benign climate, Southern California spawned arcadian communities that borrowed inspiration from European precedents, some—like Montecito and Santa Barbara—so successfully that they acquired a convincing romantic patina of history all their own.

There is no question that Montecito's spurt of growth in the early twentieth century owed a debt to architects like Reginald Johnson, Myron Hunt, and George Washington Smith and their well-heeled and sophisticated clients, many from the East Coast, who were entranced by the notion of reinventing another heritage for themselves. As the late California architectural historian David Gebhard observed, "with the majority of architects and clients of the [19]20s and [19]30s, there was an overall desire to immerse oneself in some romantically conceived episode of the distant past or to be magically transported to some exotic, faraway place." In the early part of the twentieth century, the Spanish Colonial and Mediterranean Revival architecture of large estates did in fact predominate throughout Montecito (and on the opposite coast, in West Palm Beach), and though they are appreciated by many of us as the signature of these places, the result has been a kind of architectural-cultural typecasting.

For Montecito insiders, however, the place offers a more diverse architecture. The community's public resorts and private clubs are witness to this. Reginald Johnson's 1929 Spanish Colonial Revival Biltmore Hotel is very much in the Mediterranean mode, but older resorts like the Miramar (1880, Victorian but newly reminted as "Resort Colonial") and San Ysidro Ranch (1893, California board-and-batten ranch house vernacular) are much-loved parts of Montecito's historical fabric. Next door to the Biltmore, moreover, is the Coral Casino Beach Club, a sleek, streamlined 1937 moderne building crowned with a lighthouse tower that looks straight out of Hollywood. The club has been a fixture of Montecito society ever since.

To be sure, among the community's enduring historic homes are Spanish Colonial and Mediterranean Revival examples designed by George Washington Smith (pages 179 and 247), Lutah Maria Riggs (page 265), and Francis W. Wilson (page 75), but there are also many older, less grand homes in a variety of other styles, including Victorian, Italianate, Craftsman, Tudor, and French Norman (page 197). Some of the old estate homes were eventually chopped apart and their pieces moved to create smaller, more habitable, more affordable residences (page 115), and over the years, many estate accessory outbuildings were remodeled as single-family homes (pages 141, 235, and 247). Other buildings have lost their original architectural signature to subsequent remodeling. As the mid-twentieth-century architectural scene witnessed a proliferation of modern houses, Montecito received its share of notable examples (page 61), along with work by lesser-known architects. Today one can find attractive new houses designed in both traditional Mediterranean Revival (page 223) and more contemporary styles (page 87).

The collection published here is witness not only to such architectural diversity but also to the significant contribution that sophisticated homeowners and their interior designers have brought to the equation (page 47). Quite often it has been the interior designers, rather than the architects, who have created the homes and lifestyles that exemplify the nature and spirit of present-day Montecito. Landscape designers have played a significant role as well. One of the most common elements that unite and define Montecito living is the landscape, both designed and natural. Most of the homes pictured here exhibit a focus on gardens as an extension of their interior spaces, often defining private outdoor spaces whose greenery in Southern California's mild climate can be enjoyed year-round.

The photographs and text that follow are a testament to a richer variety in Montecito's architecture and lifestyle than has typically been assumed. If "style" books purport to describe a singular character trait, *Montecito Style* is not typical. To look a little more carefully behind the hedges and closed doors of Montecito, as Firooz Zahedi and Lorie Dewhirst Porter have, is to be pleasantly surprised by this community's more personal and less predictable fabric, challenging the preconception of a common overriding Mediterranean stylistic thread.

There is no *one* Montecito style in this Valhalla of the West, which continues to be a magical place in which to live one's dream. There are, in fact, many styles to reflect these different dreams.

"I KNEW THAT IT HAD A LIFE AFTER BLUE SHAG CARPETING," says interior designer Daniel Cuevas about his first, fairly recent visit to what would ultimately become his Montecito home. Despite the offending carpet, he quips, "I could see the trees through the forest." (The trees in question, fifty-five magnificent coast live oaks , are scattered throughout the one-acre property.) Designed by an unknown architect and built in 1958, the post-and-beam structure is a masterpiece of midcentury design, with plenty of floor-to-ceiling glass walls framing outdoor views that continue to captivate Cuevas. "With all the glass, it reminds me of my childhood when I would go camping out in the forest," he says. "I'm really at the campground."

In reality, he lives in an art gallery surrounded by a campground. A dedicated collector since childhood, Cuevas has filled the residence with art and objects from his world travels, some of which had been in deep storage for years. Viewing the home as a canvas for his collections, he left the structure intact, but had it repainted in a carefully chosen gray-green tone.

THE COLLECTOR'S CAMPGROUND

"I wanted it to be the color of the trees and just blend in with the landscaping, but keep true to the architecture," he says. The landscape has become another opportunity to display his art, and several contemporary sculptures have found their way into the garden, alongside the majestic oaks.

Inside, the furnishings and art intentionally span different eras and styles. "I love modern, but I don't want to live with all modern," the designer says. Consequently, there's an eighteenth-century baker's table in the kitchen, while a seventeenth-century painting of Queen Isabella mingles happily with a pair of caribou antlers above the living room fireplace. In the dining room, a large painting by Spanish artist Fernando Iriarte is flanked by a wire totem by William de Lillo. Greeting visitors in the entryway, an abstract painting by Deborah Tarr is housed in an antique gilt frame. For Cuevas, every object possesses the power to evoke a memory. The caribou antlers were discovered at an East Hampton flea market twenty years ago and call to mind a memorable seaside weekend. The abstract painting at the entry was formerly owned by a now-departed close friend. "I have memories of everything and how it all got here," he notes.

Still, nothing is static in this household, much like his projects for clients, which continue to evolve as the peripatetic Cuevas forages for new treasures. "I'll call a client several years later and say, 'I found a great thing in Paris,'" he says with glee. The same concept applies here—as in an art gallery, objects are subject to constant rearrangement. And there's always room for more. At the moment, what he really needs is more wall space. "I have a few more things that need to come home," he says, "but it's really great to live in this environment and actually have things out of crates and up on the wall, to enjoy it every day."

The Museum of Modern Art, New York

PAGE 12 The gray-green color scheme of Daniel Cuevas's home was chosen to blend in with the surrounding landscape. "I wanted it to be the color of the trees," he says. In the dining room, a large painting by Fernando Iriarte, *La Montana Magica*, hovers over the wood dining table, flanked by a wire totem by William de Lillo. A vintage iron console discovered at a Paris flea market sits below a series of oil paintings by Marko Djuricic.

PAGES 14–15 Built in 1958, the post-and-beam structure is a masterpiece of midcentury design perfectly sited in a grove of magnificent coast live oaks. The tree branch sculpture, by Charles Arnoldi, was acquired from the estate of Michael Taylor.

PAGES 16–17 A dedicated collector since childhood, Cuevas has filled the residence with art and objects from his world travels; the furnishings and art intentionally span different eras and styles. In the living room, a seventeenth-century painting of Queen Isabella mingles happily with a pair of caribou antlers found at a flea market in East Hampton, New York.

PAGES 18–19 Floor-to-ceiling glass walls frame outdoor views that remind Cuevas of childhood camping trips. "With all the glass, it's like a campground," he says. A white Eero Saarinen Tulip table displays two decorative boxes and a string of African amber beads. An antique bronze drum fronts the linen-upholstered woven daybed. The green felt-and-bronze chicken footstool, *Little Maureen*, is by The City Girl Farm.

PAGE 20 In the entry, an abstract painting by Deborah Tarr, housed in an antique gilt frame, provides a stylistic counterpoint to a fifteenth-century carved alabaster-and-ebony box.

PAGE 21 "I love modern, but I don't want to live with all modern," the designer says. In the kitchen, an eighteenth-century walnut baker's table supports a ribbon steel sculpture by Lila Katzen. Michael McKenzie's *Culture Soup* is centered over the sink.

PAGE 22 Clerestory windows ensure privacy in the main bedroom and also provide glimpses of the outdoors while flooding the space with daylight. A cardboard chair by architect Frank Gehry is paired with a vintage cubist painting and a side table by Tony Paul.

PAGE 23 The focal point of the serene main bedroom is a luminous antique Italian *scagliola* terrestrial and zodiac map above the bed. On the left, an eighteenth-century painting of a Roman emperor in a gilded frame is paired with an antique Italian marble bust fragment.

PAGE 24 The designer's art collection extends to the garden, where a vintage wood sculpture sits between two venerable coast live oaks.

T HE FIRST THING YOU NOTICE about Lee Kirch's home is her impossibly manicured garden. Every tree, every bush, is trimmed to perfection—like sculpture. Sharp-edged hedges reign in topiary balls, lavender spikes, and exuberant olive trees; pristine paths defined by stone curbs usher you to the front door. The effect takes one's breath away, and there follows a sigh of relief. "Peaceful" is the word she most often hears from visitors.

Kirch originally viewed this relatively small Montecito residence as a project, her intent being to remodel, furnish, and sell it—and with good reason. Over the years, her homes—in Vail, St. Barts, and New York City—were so sought after that they were sold with their contents completely intact ("right down to the sheets and towels"). But this home's idyllic location—especially the extraordinary quality of light resulting from the

UNDERSTATED AESTHETIC

property's north-south orientation—captivated Kirch and ultimately persuaded her to make it her own. Architect Jane Snyder of Mosaic Architects & Interiors was responsible for interpreting Kirch's design ideas, translating them into plans, and obtaining the requisite approvals and permits.

The result is an environment dancing with light. In the kitchen, a cupola admits indirect rays from above, and the gray marble-topped island and countertops below lend a cool, shady counterpoint. Adjoining the kitchen, the intimate dining area, surrounded on three sides by tall windows and glass doors, feels like a solarium. Light is also at play in the living room, where the gray marble-faced fireplace is flanked by rectangular casements and centered under a high clerestory window. In the bedroom, tall mirrored doors reflect the French doors leading out to the adjacent multilayered green-on-green garden.

The overall color scheme—inspired by Swedish Gustavian decor—is a series of calm neutrals that change tone as light passes through the myriad windows that offer outdoor views from virtually every room. There are no window coverings to be seen because, as Kirch says, "the outside is my color." Furnishings are minimal but exquisite. It's an aesthetic honed by experience and a gradual evolution toward a simpler, less cluttered lifestyle. "I'll walk into a room, and I'll think, this is just too much stuff, I've got too many books scattered or too many things, and I'll weed it all out again and try to get back to the bones of it."

PAGE 26   Light floods the dining area adjacent to the kitchen. Surrounded on three sides by tall windows and glass doors, the intimate space feels like a solarium. The home's furnishings are minimal but exquisite, and there are no window coverings to be seen. "The outside is my color," says Kirch.

PAGE 28   The angular design of the house is mirrored by the garden, where topiary trees and hedges have been painstakingly trimmed.

PAGE 29   Pristine paths flanked by box hedges lead to the front door. The surrounding dense foliage leads the eye upward toward the Santa Ynez mountains in the background.

PAGES 30–31   In the living room, a treasured European landscape painting is centered above the gray marble-faced fireplace, which is flanked by tall rectangular casements. An eighteenth-century marble-topped commode hosts a vintage carved wood *santos* depicting St. Francis of Assisi.

PAGE 32 The overall color scheme—inspired by Swedish Gustavian decor—is a series of calm neutrals. The focal point of the dining room is an antique Swedish wood desk from Country House Antiques that has been repurposed as a sideboard.

PAGE 33 In the kitchen, a cupola lets in indirect light from above, and the gray marble-topped island and countertops below are a dark counterpoint. The built-in shelves display a collection of antique ironstone pottery.

PAGES 34–35 In the garden, topiary balls mingle with lavender spikes. A sharply trimmed box hedge provides a verdant background for an inviting wicker chaise longue placed alongside a sandstone-edged square fountain. "Peaceful" is the word Kirch most often hears from visitors to her home.

PAGE 36 An outdoor dining room surrounded by tall leafy hedges features curved wrought-iron benches from William Laman and a vintage fountain reclaimed from a nearby Montecito estate.

E VERY TIME SOMETHING COMES INTO THIS TINY SPACE something has to go out," says Hanna Foraker of her jewel-box aerie perched atop a two-car garage. Enforcing such a rule, however, has proved challenging for this avid collector of beautiful objects. Indeed, the space is a virtual *Wunderkammer* of collectibles, including "anything that's staghorn" in honor of her upbringing in the Bavarian Alps. Antlers adorn tabletops and mingle with greenery on the sideboard; there's even a stash of staghorn cutlery.

Widowed since 2011, Foraker has spent the past decade editing her collection to "a fraction" of what she used to have. "Once upon a time I had a vast collection of Staffordshire [figurines]," she says fondly, "because a stark piece of English brown oak with one piece of Staffordshire will bring that piece of furniture alive." Even so, there are plenty of treasures to ponder. It's a space that invites your eyes to dance.

The walls are adorned with an intricate puzzle of immaculately framed vintage wonders: a combination of intricate botanicals by Basilius Besler, detailed architectural renderings by Giovanni Battista Falda, and hand-colored bird's-eye views of English estates by Johannes Kip. Among her favorite pieces are the exquisite antique wood tea caddies that nestle in corners, sharing space with rows of gleaming nineteenth-century pewter bowls from England. Formerly a lawn bowler, Foraker even collects lawn balls, often placing them in abandoned bird nests for a witty display. "I've never been a Minimalist," she concedes. "I've always liked not clutter per se, but just enough to where there's an interest, where you can jump around and go from eighteenth-century pottery to little twentieth-century bronzes."

THE BEDSIT

Admittedly, entertaining guests in such small quarters can be challenging. "One 'repairs' from living room to dining room all within five hundred [square] feet, if that," she says with a laugh. But the lucky few who obtain entrance are undoubtedly entranced by their surroundings. And despite Foraker's determination to continue editing her prized possessions, one senses the hunt is not over yet, as she confides: "You know, I'm currently looking at another pair of Besler botanicals that I just covet."

PAGE 38 A *Wunderkammer* of collectibles, Hanna Foraker's jewel-box aerie is perched atop a two-car garage. In one corner, a portion of her collection of framed antique botanicals surrounds a late-nineteenth-century architectural staircase sample. Immediately above, an eighteenth-century Georgian mahogany quarter-round cabinet supports an antique headless wood *santos*. "I've never been a Minimalist," Foraker admits.

PAGES 40–41 The walls of the tiny space display an intricate puzzle of immaculately framed vintage wonders, including several hand-colored bird's-eye views of English estates by Johannes Kip. On the center table are several prized antique wood tea caddies along with an abandoned bird's nest.

PAGES 42–43 Entertaining guests in such small quarters can be challenging. "One 'repairs' from the living room to dining room all within five hundred feet, if that," Foraker says with a laugh. Formerly a lawn bowler, Foraker also collects lawn balls.

PAGE 44 Nineteenth-century pewter bowls from England and more antique wood tea caddies adorn the sideboard. Several bronze dachshund sculptures by Joy Kroeger Beckner share space with a portrait of Foraker's own beloved dog, Annie, painted by Mary Griggs.

W ORLD-RENOWNED INTERIOR DESIGNER John Saladino was a teenager when he first visited Montecito during a family road trip, and he was smitten. At the time, his illustrious forty-year career lay ahead, during which he would design and inhabit several astounding residences in New York City while presiding over a twenty-acre estate in Connecticut. It was not until the end of the 1980s that the designer ultimately moved west and claimed Montecito as home, his wicked sense of humor exemplified by the nickname assigned to his current abode: The Departure Lounge.

The repository of a lifetime of collecting, the residence—originally built in the 1960s and designed by John W. Bancroft and architect Hugh M. O'Connell Jr.—has a clean, almost modernist style. Its contents represent a masterstroke of ruthless editing that leaves only those possessions the designer cannot live without, items deemed precious not only for their value but also for their ability to conjure their owner's memories. Among them is an extraordinary marble sculpture of a herm at the entrance to the living room. It is considered especially rare

RESTRAINED ELEGANCE

not just because of its age (dating from either ancient Greece, 200 BCE, or Rome, 200 CE) but because its form is obviously female, while most herms are decidedly male. Directly on axis from the sculpture—at the end of the central corridor—sits another treasure: a sixteenth-century Italian carved wood chest featuring the labors of Hercules, upon which rests the very first Saladino-designed glass lamp, which is still in production today.

A large architectural fragment from Rome's Baths of Caracalla, suspended high above the living room fireplace also made the rigorous cut, as did a monumental bronze candlestick ("probably fifteenth century") the designer purchased furtively in Paris during a buying trip with a client. The dining room table boasts a cherished collection of antique silver candlesticks in the shape of Corinthian columns, gifts from his beloved late wife, Virginia, who "seduced me into becoming a silver addict," Saladino says.

Hallmarks of Saladino's design aesthetic are notable throughout—from the wonderfully muted wall colors to the carefully calibrated pairing of antique pieces with furniture of his own design. The overall effect is luxury invigorated by the occasional dash of whimsy. A case in point is the dining room's tray ceiling, embellished with delicate grisaille branches hand painted by local artist Colette Cosentino, featuring the portrait of a small mouse perched over the double doors leading to the kitchen.

The ultimate essence of these inspiring spaces is the manifestation of a gracious lifestyle, where beauty, comfort, and function are carefully intertwined. As Saladino himself declares, "I think that a house should be a sanctuary where you close the door on reality to make your own world, your own reality. It should have the most careful editing of what makes you happy. Home is a place that you edit to perfection against the onslaught of the real world."

PAGE 46   John Saladino created a theatrical setting for his pool area, where a pergola on two marble columns rising from the water acts as a stage, perfectly framing a scenic view of the distant Santa Ynez mountains.

PAGES 48–49   The great room captures the hallmark's of Saladino's design aesthetic, a carefully calibrated mixture of antique pieces with furniture of his own design. An ottoman covered with a nineteenth-century Persian silk tablecloth centers the room, on axis with Saladino's Cromwell settee bench, which is flanked by four watercolor architectural elevations by Sir John Soane. A converted candlestick lamp on the right illuminates Saladino's Trunk chair.

PAGE 50   A fragment from Rome's Baths of Caracalla is suspended high above the fireplace, attesting to Saladino's affinity for antiquity. In the corner, two eighteenth-century English columns are paired with a Venetian Byzantine column.

PAGE 51   A folding screen covered in nineteenth-century Zuber grisaille wallpaper provides a dramatic backdrop for the designer's treasured ancient marble herm sculpture.

54

PAGES 52–53 The dining room's tray ceiling is embellished with delicate grisaille branches hand painted by artist Colette Cosentino. Saladino's Villa chairs surround the dining table, which boasts a collection of antique silver candlesticks in the shape of Corinthian columns. Adding a dash of whimsy, sunglasses adorn a nineteenth-century plaster bust of Sir Francis Drake.

PAGE 54 The library's fireplace mantel displays a fourteenth-century travel set of ivory knife and fork handles and a carved fragment from a Roman sarcophagus.

PAGE 55 In the wood-paneled library, a large abstract that Saladino painted in 2011 centers the room, which also contains a collection of the designer's furniture, including his Shelter sofa, Trunk chair, and collapsible tripod Terazzo table.

PAGE 56 The serene wood-paneled guest bedroom features an eighteenth-century Italian officer's campaign bed made of hand-forged steel.

PAGE 57 The home's central corridor leads to a sixteenth-century Italian carved wood chest featuring the labors of Hercules, on which rest a collection of ancient Korean ginger jars and the very first Saladino-designed glass lamp, which is still in production today. Giovanni Battista Piranesi's eighteenth-century plan of the Campus Martius hangs above the ensemble.

PAGE 58 In the main bedroom, an Italian carved wood marriage chest supports a curated display of favorite objects—cricket cages from Japan and a collection of antique wood boxes—all gathered under a nineteenth-century plaster acanthus leaf relief from the French Academy used to instruct students of the Beaux-Arts school.

INSPIRED BY ITS DARING CONCRETE AND GLASS COMPOSITION and equally audacious below-ground setting, architecture aficionados have admired this stunning residence since its completion in 1974. But for most local residents, this extraordinary home remains unknown, literally hidden in a canyon hillside above Santa Barbara.

The namesake son of an architect who helped define California residential style in the 1920s and 1930s, Roland Coate Jr. looked to Southern California's sprawling freeway system as the impetus for his groundbreaking design; in his view, freeway construction was the local vernacular architecture of the time. Coate was also well aware of other architects creating with concrete, having both worked for master architects I. M. Pei and Marcel Breuer on the East Coast and witnessed the construction of Le Corbusier's iconic chapel in Ronchamp, France. Using concrete was also a pragmatic choice for the architect, given its fireproof character and the home's location in a high fire zone.

Yet even today, few clients would welcome a house that some—although certainly not the architect—might describe as brutalist. But Nancy and Jesse Alexander, the original owners, were hardly ordinary clients. A professional photographer, Jesse traveled the world photographing European motorcar races such as France's 24 Hours of Le Mans and Italy's Mille Miglia. Nancy, a stage actress, was equally well traveled and worked in the design field.

THE SCULPTURAL HOME

Given their sophistication, Coate's suggestion to build a home unlike anything in the area was met with enthusiasm and excitement.

The couple embraced the project wholeheartedly. Nancy worked closely with Coate to establish the programmatic details for the seven-thousand-square-foot building, while Jesse documented its construction with his 1974 movie *Mud House*, a cult film for architecture students to this day. The film's depiction of workers erecting the tall wood forms, aligning and tying off the rebar, and performing the challenging physical choreography of the concrete pour is an indelible reminder of the complexity behind its design and construction.

Despite the passage of more than four decades, the residence retains its capacity to astonish. A winding driveway leads to the crest of a hill, where an expansive lawn hosts three chimneys and a circular watchtower—a surreal, Minimalist landscape that faces the panoramic coastline view. The house sits below, accessed by a red brick staircase that descends to a walled courtyard, where a long glass facade introduces the front entrance.

The current owner has taken advantage of the expansive interior by installing large-scale artworks that complement the building's monumental proportions. Circular fireplaces and pillars serve to break the structure's rigidity, inserting rhythm into the overall circulation. The interior spaces are surprisingly intimate, each radiating outward toward the horizon. The living room is tastefully furnished with Michael Taylor's jewel-toned seating, wood tables crafted by Rusty Dobbs of Ghostown Woodworks, and paintings by Bill Whiskey Tjapaltjarri and April Gornik. These elements provide a soft counterpoint to the raw concrete walls that are artworks themselves, each bearing the imprint of wood grain patterns from the hand-built forms that created them.

A Bo Bartlett painting dominates an adjacent game area, its James Perse table topped with metal lamps from Blackman Cruz. The dining room's massive marble table, flanked by vintage leather chairs, is one-of-a-kind, and a painting by Eric Fischl completes the ensemble. The main bedroom is an especially cozy retreat, with pieces by Terry Winters and Susan Rothenberg gracing the walls and a bronze sculpture by Ruth Vollmer enhancing an antique table. The primary event, made possible by the concrete armature, is the spectacular view that is conspicuous from nearly every room.

PAGE 60 Despite the passage of time, this stunning 1974 all-concrete residence designed by architect Roland Coate Jr. retains its capacity to astonish.

PAGES 62–63 Built into the hillside, the home has panoramic views from nearly every room. The architect had witnessed the construction of Le Corbusier's concrete chapel in Ronchamp, France, and was also inspired by freeway construction in Southern California.

PAGES 64–65 On the hilltop, an expansive lawn hosts three chimneys and a circular watchtower, creating a surreal, Minimalist landscape. The house sits below, accessed by a red brick staircase that descends into a walled courtyard.

PAGES 66–67 The current owner has taken advantage of the expansive interior by installing large-scale artworks that complement the building's monumental proportions. The living room is tastefully furnished with Michael Taylor's jewel-toned seating, wood tables crafted by Rusty Dobbs of Ghostown Woodworks, and paintings by Bill Whiskey Tjapaltjarri and April Gornik.

PAGE 68 A Bo Bartlett painting dominates the game area, its James Perse table topped with metal lamps from Blackman Cruz.

PAGE 69 The dining room's massive marble table, flanked by vintage leather chairs, is original, and a painting by Eric Fischl completes the ensemble.

PAGES 70–71 The main bedroom is a welcoming retreat, with pieces by Terry Winters and Susan Rothenberg gracing the walls. Near the circular fireplace, an antique table hosts a bronze sculpture by Ruth Vollmer.

PAGE 72 Two poolside armchairs on the red brick terrace encourage relaxed contemplation of the spectacular coastline.

WITH ITS SERENE SYMMETRY, graceful proportions, and formal garden setting, this Montecito villa palpably evokes the Classical details of Italian Renaissance architecture. The architect, Francis W. Wilson, was trained in the Beaux-Arts style and designed several public buildings that continue to define the character of downtown Santa Barbara today, including the railway station, the main public library, and the Santa Barbara Museum of Art.

Built in 1915, the property was in a neglected state when acquired by its current owners in 2005. They lovingly restored the century-old building and carefully reworked several additions that had been made to the building over the years to better reflect the villa's overall style. In doing so, they proved neoclassical style can successfully, even brilliantly, coexist with cutting-

A BALANCING ACT

edge art. Traditional upholstered furniture mingles easily with large-scale contemporary paintings and sculpture; the original wood-paneled living room has been painted an eye-popping shade of shiny peacock blue; and the gilded ceiling in the dining room casts a golden glow. Local architect Bob Easton helped ensure the home's overall architectural integrity, and designer Marion Gregston's exquisite taste and professional eye enhanced the interior decor. The overall result is grand yet intimate, formal without being stuffy.

It's also child friendly. "Our children have loved it," says the owner. "Most of their childhood has been here. There's lots of places to hide or run around. They loved the idea that they could do a lot of different things, build forts in the living room, and that there weren't any real rules other than just be careful and mindful, respectful of the art and the house." The family's four energetic dogs are enthusiastic as well but appear less circumspect about their impressive surroundings.

As is true throughout Southern California, much of life here is lived outdoors. With the expert assistance of local landscape architects Sam W. Maphis IV and Stacy Fausset, the villa's extensive gardens were thoughtfully renovated into a series of outdoor rooms. Two towering eucalyptus trees frame the portico, from which the formal garden spreads out seamlessly like a living carpet. Tall hedges cordon off certain areas, where site-specific artworks have been judiciously placed for thoughtful contemplation. "Our art collection has found its way outside as well," the owner notes, "which is really fun." You could say it took a twenty-first-century art collection to bring a twentieth-century house back to life.

PAGE 74 The graceful entryway of this handsome residence features a grand staircase that leads to the private areas of the home. Near the front door, a collection of blue-and-white porcelain commands attention.

PAGES 76–77 Serene symmetry and graceful proportions characterize this Italianate villa. Built in 1915, it was designed by architect Francis W. Wilson, who also designed several public buildings in downtown Santa Barbara. The property was in a neglected state when acquired by its current owners, who lovingly restored the building and reworked several additions to better reflect the villa's overall style.

PAGES 78–79 The owners have proved that Neoclassical style can coexist with cutting-edge art, as evidenced by the contemporary pieces strategically placed along the hallway adjacent to the home's entrance.

PAGES 80–81 In the living room, the original wood paneling has been painted an eye-popping shade of shiny peacock blue, and traditional upholstered furniture mingles easily with large-scale contemporary paintings.

PAGE 82 Rich textiles and dark blue walls are paired with large-scale artwork in the TV room.

PAGE 83 The gilded ceiling of the dining room casts a golden glow; a contemporary photograph hovers over the fireplace.

PAGE 84 The loggia, covered in greenery, provides an alternative outdoor dining space. The shattered mirror pieces were designed by one of the owners.

A ESTHETICALLY, FOR MY OWN HOUSE, I wanted to do something that I hadn't been asked to do by clients," says architect William Hefner about the Montecito home he designed for his family. Originally conceived as a weekend getaway from their Hancock Park residence in Los Angeles, the idea was to create a compound similar to a hotel, where an outdoor ramble might be required to reach the dining room from one's sleeping quarters. In part, this unique layout was dictated by the majestic presence of a grouping of two-hundred-year-old oak trees located on the site, as well as the magnificent mountain views to the north. "I felt like the house should be somewhat subservient to the exterior spaces," Hefner recalls.

The discovery of large deposits of Santa Barbara sandstone during the land-grading process provoked significant design changes to thoughtfully take advantage of that fortuitous find. The excavated stones were used to create retaining walls in the garden and, later, to clad several of the buildings, a treatment inspired by the work of Bay Area architect Bernard Maybeck. "Eventually, the house became a dialogue between stone buildings and wood buildings," Hefner says. The use of two exterior materials also visually delineates the public and private areas of the residence. The expansive great

CALM AND CURATED

room, comprising the kitchen, dining room, and living room, is covered primarily in stone, while the bedroom wing is clad in wood. A glass-enclosed breezeway separates the two spaces, and one has the sensation of briefly stepping into nature when traversing between the public and private realms. The wood-clad pool house that doubles as guest quarters is a few steps away from the stone-clad gym with its stunning outdoor shower. Wall-sized steel-and-glass windows and metal roofs are common elements in this gathering of buildings.

Hefner's deliberate choice of a neutral, tone-on-tone color scheme throughout ensures the home's outdoor surroundings are not upstaged. "Color is sometimes a distraction," he notes. The interior plaster, cedar millwork, walnut cabinets, and flooring flow together in visual harmony, along with the vintage lighting and simple, unlacquered brass fixtures. The overall effect is modern without the risk of being dated.

Given the architect's starting point for the project, it comes as no surprise that the garden is the central element. The pool, outdoor seating, and guest areas all take advantage of the spectacular mountain views, and the stately oaks provide dappled shade. The stone walls and native plants and grasses provide a textural contrast to the lawn area that parallels the pool. A vegetable garden and citrus grove edge the northern border of the property.

Much to his amusement, Hefner's own home has proved extremely popular with clients. "It surprises me because it wasn't my goal to make something that people would be interested in," he says with a smile. Of course, talented architects like Hefner never duplicate their designs exactly. As he notes, "they become like a second or third cousin rather than a brother or a twin."

PAGE 86 The entryway of architect William Hefner's weekend getaway is clad in Santa Barbara sandstone excavated on site during the grading process. Stone cladding visually delineates the public from the private areas of the residence, which are clad in wood.

PAGES 88–89 Hefner deliberately chose a neutral tone-on-tone color scheme to ensure the home's outdoor surroundings would not be upstaged. In the great room, the fireplace's sandstone cladding reaches all the way to the ceiling. The wood credenza and low-slung chairs are vintage.

PAGE 90 A vintage sconce (one of a pair) is centered over a Minimalist console in the billiard room.

PAGE 91 The billiard room—with its restored 1950s bronze-and-walnut pool table—doubles as Hefner's office.

PAGE 92 The main bedroom has its own fireplace and tall glass doors that provide views of the garden. The neutral furnishings, including a custom parchment cabinet, seem to reflect light.

PAGE 93 The shower in the primary bathroom has a private view of the garden. The brass sconces are vintage.

PAGES 94–95 The home's layout was dictated by a group of oak trees on the site. Hefner's design creates a compound similar to a hotel, where an outdoor ramble might be required to reach the dining room from one's sleeping quarters.

PAGES 96–97 The poolside seating area has a spectacular view of the mountains. Stone walls and native grasses provide a textural contrast to the expanse of lawn that parallels the pool.

PAGE 98 An enormous outdoor fireplace with outdoor seating is flanked by tall steel-and-glass walls that outline the interior corridor between the public and private spaces of the home.

THIS SLEEK MODERNIST VILLA—designed by an unknown architect—was surprisingly once a Victorian-style home, completely transformed in the early 1900s after its owners returned from an inspiring European jaunt. The long-ago renovation also featured an elegant garden (likely designed by renowned local landscape architect Lockwood de Forest Jr.) and an outdoor theater replete with a below-ground orchestra pit. By the time its current owners, Tammy and Kim Hughes, acquired it in 2016, the property had been unoccupied for years. "We didn't quite realize how many potential purchasers were advised not to take it on," Kim admits. Thankfully, the two recognized the building's potential. As Tammy says, "It was love at first sight."

Even so, the restoration process was arduous. "It didn't seem like that big of a deal," Tammy acknowledges, "until they started pulling off the roof and pulling the walls apart and lifting up the house to do a new foundation." The original floor plan was left largely intact but for a kitchen expansion and an added powder room on the main floor. Tammy still marvels at the building's design—especially the four lightwells that effectively illuminate the lower floors during the day, deeming them "so smart and so thoughtful." Fortunately, she insisted on retaining and refinishing nearly all the villa's original doors and windows, a decision that ensured the building's modernist design retained its authenticity.

ECLECTIC SPIRIT

As an interior designer and owner of Emerald Eye Designs, Tammy was unfazed at the prospect of furnishing a residence exceeding eleven thousand square feet. Kim was also undeterred by the project's size, having summered in England as a child at his grandparents' stately home, Barton Abbey, with his famous uncle, Ian Fleming (author of the James Bond novels). In fact, the gray antique settle in the kitchen "is very close to what is at Barton," according to Kim. The kitchen's centerpiece, a cobalt-blue Aga stove, is set against the brick backside of the dining room fireplace (one of seven in the villa).

The home's wonderfully eclectic interiors are also the result of the couple's frequent pilgrimages to flea markets and auction houses of the world. A massive silver, faux-taxidermy rhino head presides over the dining room table, a whimsical trophy offset by a large nude portrait by contemporary artist Lu Cong. In the living room, a large narrative painting from 1915 contrasts with a carved wood saint from the 1800s. An intricate antique mirror tops the minimalist living room fireplace, which is flanked by two salmon-hued velvet couches favored by the family canines.

The garden was another challenge the couple embraced. The palm tree– and column-lined terraces leading down to the outdoor theater were restored, and four antique Italian commedia dell'arte statutes, formerly in residence at a Los Angeles estate, were installed as bemused sentries awaiting performances from the still-extant orchestra pit and stage.

PAGE 100 The wonderfully eclectic interiors in this home are the result of its owners' frequent pilgrimages to flea markets and auction houses all over the world. In the living room, vibrant chairs vie for attention with a framed collection of exotic butterflies.

PAGES 102–103 This sleek modernist villa, designed by an unknown architect, was once a Victorian-style home that was completely transformed in the early 1900s. By the time its current owners, Tammy and Kim Hughes, acquired it in 2016, the property had been unoccupied for years. The restoration process was arduous but satisfying. "The goal was to honor what was here," says Tammy.

PAGE 104 The owners restored the garden with its palm- and column-lined terraces leading down to an outdoor theater. One walled terrace features a firepit fashioned from a cauldron.

PAGE 105 A huge palm tree provides a dramatic backdrop for an outdoor dining room in the garden.

PAGES 106-107 As an interior designer, owner Tammy Hughes was unfazed by the prospect of furnishing a residence exceeding eleven thousand square feet. The entry, displaying furnishings and art from a variety of eras, beckons visitors toward a cozy fireplace at the far end of the space.

PAGE 108 Two vintage leather chairs flank a small fireplace—one of seven in the residence—located at the end of the expansive foyer.

PAGE 109 In the living room, where everyone tends to gather, an intricate antique mirror tops the fireplace, which is flanked by two salmon-hued velvet couches. A pair of antique convex mirrors adds to the symmetry, and framed family photographs share space with African sculptures.

PAGE 110 The kitchen's centerpiece, a cobalt-blue Aga stove, is set against the brick backside of the dining room fireplace.

PAGE 111 A massive silver faux rhino head presides over the dining room table, a whimsical trophy offset by a nude portrait by contemporary artist Lu Cong.

PAGE 112 After much research, Tammy and Kim suspect their elegant classical garden was likely designed by renowned local landscape architect Lockwood de Forest Jr., who was responsible for similar designs for other large Montecito estates. An orchestra pit and outdoor stage still exist on the property.

"T HIS HOUSE HAS SEEN MORE CELEBRITIES than the commissary at Twentieth Century Fox," quips Allan Glaser about his home, an antiques-filled domicile he shared with his late husband, actor Tab Hunter. Indeed, the couple's social circle was a like round robin of classic silver screen opening credits: Don Murray, Jane Russell, Rod Taylor, Richard Widmark, and next-door neighbors Suzy Parker and Bradford Dillman. "There was a communality that we had; we all lived here, we didn't talk movies, but everybody had an interesting history," Glaser says.

This residence is actually a segment from a neighboring George Washington Smith–designed estate that was detached in the late 1940s and relocated to create a separate home, and the intricate wood paneling Smith painstakingly detailed still graces the fireplace wall in the living room. Purchased by Glaser and Hunter in 1994, the two made a few interior improvements while maintaining the building's existing footprint. "We wanted to take it back to its glory," says Glaser. "We didn't want to change it

HUNTER'S LODGE

into something else." But the now-magnificent garden, with its stately view of the mountains, was lovingly created from scratch.

Hunter, a lifelong equestrian and an avid collector of antiques who ran his own shop in Beverly Hills in the 1960s, was largely responsible for the eclectic interior decor. His bedroom walls display a passion for horses, both real and imagined, and also include the championship ribbons he garnered on the show circuit. Notably lacking, however, is any trace of Hollywood, apart from the leather chairs in the entryway (once owned by Rock Hudson) and the dining room table (a gift from Vincent Price). "No movie memorabilia was allowed in this house," notes Glaser firmly. "When Tab finished his career, he walked away from it and went on with life."

The life of Tab Hunter has, of course, been the subject of public interest from the moment his film career began in 1950; he was actively promoted by studio publicity departments and relentlessly pursued by movie tabloids for years. His best-selling 2005 autobiography, *Tab Hunter Confidential: The Making of a Movie Star*, and *Tab Hunter Confidential*, the award-winning 2015 documentary produced by Glaser, revealed the disconnect between fame and reality, and the psychic toll public scrutiny can impose.

Luckily, the story has an actual Hollywood happy ending. After meeting at Twentieth Century Fox in the 1980s, when Glaser was director of feature film acquisitions, Hunter and Glaser became business partners in a film production company (their film *Lust in the Dust*, starring Hunter, is a cult classic) as well as partners in life. They were together thirty-six years, twenty-five of which were spent in their Montecito home. In the end, Glaser says, "It was the best gift Tab gave me, to bring me up here and then settle down here with me. Because now I've grown into what the Montecito lifestyle is, and can appreciate it, and I'm much less Hollywood and much more Montecito."

PAGE 114 An intimate dining area resulted from enclosing an outdoor loggia at the home of Tab Hunter and Allan Glaser. "Tab and I used to sit and have dinner here every night," Glaser says. The couple's social circle was like a round robin of classic silver screen opening credits.

PAGES 116–17 The Spanish Colonial Revival residence is actually a segment from a neighboring George Washington Smith–designed estate that was detached in the late 1940s and relocated to create a separate home. Hunter and Glaser acquired the property in 1994.

PAGE 118 The leafy garden, with its tall hedges and statuary, was created by Hunter and Glaser from scratch and transformed into a private oasis for contemplation.

PAGE 119 The chic entry foyer, with its black-and-white marble tile, includes an antique leather chair (one of a pair) formerly owned by Rock Hudson.

PAGES 120–21 Hunter was an avid collector of antiques—he even ran his own shop in Beverly Hills—and was responsible for the home's eclectic interior decor. "Tab had great taste from living around the world," says Glaser. "He was just an elegant man." The wall behind the fireplace retains the intricate carved oak paneling designed by architect George Washington Smith.

PAGES 122–23 The centerpiece of the elegant dining room is a dramatic antique tapestry; the dining table was a gift from Vincent Price. "No movie memorabilia was allowed in this house," says Glaser. "When Tab finished his career, he walked away from it and went on with life."

PAGES 124–25 A lifelong equestrian, Hunter's bedroom walls display his passion for horses. "The only photographs you'll see of Tab are with his horses," says Glaser, "not Tab with Sophia Loren, or Lana Turner, or Debbie Reynolds, or Natalie Wood."

PAGE 126 A detail of Hunter's bedroom captures a collection of wood *santos* gathered by the couple on various trips. "Tab was religious," Glaser notes, "and he loved his *santos* collection."

W ITHOUT A DOUBT, this newly built estate occupies one of the most stunning beachfront locations in Montecito. Situated at the tip of a secluded point—a natural outcropping shared by only a handful of other homes on an exclusive stretch of beach—it is also, given the ever-increasing restrictions on coastal development in California, likely the last residence of its size to be built within a stone's throw of the ocean. Because the construction footprint was dictated by the skeleton foundation of an unbuilt house existing on the property, its owners lovingly dub it the "ultimate house of compromise."

Embracing this definitive concrete footprint in the sand, local firm Winick Architects successfully adapted the home's architectural style and program to fit the owners' specific needs. Although a fourteen-thousand-square-foot structure can hardly be termed a "beach house," the owners eschewed stuffy formalism for the casual feel of open spaces with direct ocean access. As a result, an expansive space paralleling the beachfront combines living and dining

BEACHSIDE SPLENDOR

rooms into one space, with floor-to-ceiling steel-framed glass doors opening onto a spacious loggia. An intimate library to the west of the living room has glass doors leading to the beach on one side and access to a Moroccan style garden on the other. Even the state-of-the-art gym, with its circular staircase leading to the cardio equipment, steam shower, and sauna above, faces the ocean. Upstairs, the primary bedroom stands opposite the horizon, on axis with its own private terrace. "Upstairs feels like you're on a ship because you can see the view through two different sides of the house," says the client. Architect Barry Winick describes the home's overall style as "very French Riviera making its way to bits of Italy."

Renowned interior designer Richard Shapiro provided valuable advice early on, accompanying the client on a buying trip to Italy to obtain several reclaimed elements, including the dining room fireplace, the library floor, and several columns that were integrated into the project. Mark D. Sikes later picked up the design baton, adding textiles, window dressings, furniture, and accessories to the mix. Robert Adams of EarthKnower Studio was responsible for landscape design and managed to create a natural but seamless transition between the home and beachfront. The ultimate result is a home that, despite its monumental size, truly fits the family that owns it.

PAGE 128 Floor-to-ceiling glass doors open onto a spacious loggia whose graceful arches frame a view of the ocean. "It's a very casual house in many ways," says the owner. "We sit at those long tables and have pizza, and we can see the kids wherever they are."

PAGES 130–31 The home's front elevation is traditional, but cloying symmetry has been avoided in the placement and size of the windows. The architect, Barry Winick, describes the residence's overall style as "very French Riviera making its way to bits of Italy."

PAGES 132–33 Although a fourteen-thousand-square-foot structure can hardly be termed a "beach house," the owners eschewed stuffy formalism for the casual feel of open spaces with direct ocean access. An expansive space paralleling the beachfront combines living and dining rooms into one space.

PAGES 134–35 Enjoying one of the most stunning beachfront locations in Montecito, the home is situated at the tip of a secluded point, a natural outcropping shared by only a handful of other homes on an exclusive stretch of beach.

PAGE 136 In the entry hallway, a large vintage textile backs a carved wood sideboard topped with a collection of green pottery.

PAGE 137 "It doesn't feel like a beach house," says the owner, "but there's a view from almost every room." Blue-and-white tiles flank steel-framed glass doors and an expansive vista.

PAGE 138 An outdoor dining area with herringbone brick, colorful tiles, and inlaid furniture has a Moroccan vibe.

OCCASIONALLY ONE DISCOVERS A HOME with interiors so well conceived one wishes the owner would establish a design business. Such is the case with this residential compound, a delightful cluster of buildings including a majestic stone carriage house, a blacksmith's cottage, and a rustic wood-sided barn. Dating from the late nineteenth century, these historic buildings are thought to have been part of the Waterman estate, one of the earliest grand Montecito estates. The current owners, who hail from South Africa, originally acquired the carriage house for their own home and obtained the adjoining acreage, with the barn and cottage (now the pool–guest house), a dozen years later.

The magnificent carriage house, built with local stone, lies at the center of the property. A beautiful two-story building, it has been repurposed as comfy living quarters. Massive wood beams span the ceilings, and a large fireplace sits at the center of the main room, with a series of whimsical, carved animals prancing across its mantel. An intimate wood-

HERITAGE PRESERVED

paneled dining room, accessed through Gothic-style wood doors, boasts its own marble-faced fireplace. The beautiful staircase leading to the second floor boasts a delicate ironwork balustrade, an artwork in itself.

But the true heart of the property is the simple pitched-roof barn. "I find this the most soulful, beautiful building to be in," says one of the owners, who was responsible for its inspired interiors. Originally intended as a playhouse for the grandchildren, the barn space evolved over time into living quarters, although the process itself was arduous. Local building requirements mandated relocating the structure within the current setback zone, a task achieved by architecture firm Appleton Partners. The derelict floor and interior walls were carefully replaced with wide planks of reclaimed Douglas fir. Fortunately, the original ceilings remained intact.

The perfect scale of the barn's great room makes one feel immediately at ease, as does the wonderful mix of furnishings. The interior design reveals a true genius for blending antique English Georgian furniture with exotic handmade textiles and art from South Africa. A magnificent collection of colorful ceramics from Ardmore, an artist community in the KwaZulu-Natal Midlands of South Africa, is on view throughout the space. Ardmore fabric also adorns the Hepplewhite-style dining room chairs: an inspiring combination. In the guest bedroom, traditional Basotho blankets with a graphic corncob motif keep company with the turtles, rabbits, and fish cavorting on the fabric headboard and bedspread made from vintage, West African hand-woven cotton. The overall feeling is casual elegance, a sophisticated simplicity that invites close inspection and serene contemplation.

The garden, also designed by the talented owner, surrounds the various buildings like an embrace. Pathways and allées lead to outdoor rooms, and mature oak and olive trees mingle with silvery Australian and South African plants. From the pool house, a bright indigo swath of agapanthus blooms is visible over the leafy green hedge.

PAGE 140 A nineteenth-century carriage house, thought to be part of one of the earliest grand Montecito estates, has been repurposed as living quarters. The beautiful staircase leading to the second floor boasts a delicate iron balustrade that is an artwork in itself.

PAGES 142–43 A carefully manicured garden leads up to the stone carriage house.

PAGE 144 Inside, the original stone walls have been left intact. A small wood-framed window is surrounded by a collection of art and books gathered on floating wood plank shelves.

PAGE 145 The intimate wood-paneled dining room is accessed through Gothic-style wood doors and has a marble-faced fireplace.

PAGE 146 The true heart of the property is a simple pitched-roof wood barn, which the owners originally intended as a playhouse for the grandchildren. It has evolved over time into living quarters.

PAGE 147 The owners replaced the barn's derelict floor and and interior walls with wide planks of reclaimed Douglas fir. A rustic interior staircase, also clad in fir, provides access to the barn's second floor.

PAGES 148–49 The perfect scale of the barn's great room makes one feel immediately at ease, as does the wonderful mix of furnishings. The interior design reveals a true genius for blending antique English Georgian furniture with textiles and contemporary art from South Africa.

PAGE 150 In the bedroom, a colorful Suzani textile adorns the wood four-poster bed.

PAGE 151 In the blacksmith's cottage, a traditional green-and-orange Basotho blanket with graphic motifs decorates the bed.

PAGE 152 In the barn's great room, built-in wood shelves display a colorful collection of South African ceramics.

PAGE 153 The central island of the barn's kitchen is illuminated by a series of four dramatic pendant lights made from South African sisal.

PAGES 154–55 A leafy pergola provides shade for an outdoor dining table, with the stone carriage house as a backdrop.

PAGE 156 The well-tended garden surrounding the barn is an inspired combination of mature oak and olive trees combined with Australian and South African plants. The rustic outdoor dining table, with its vintage metal chairs, provides a perfect setting for al fresco entertaining.

T HE DAZZLING VISUAL IMPACT of this midcentury modern residence is the result of a convergence of creative minds: the architect's and the owners'. The architect, Jack Lionel Warner, was known for his elegant custom home designs, and his firm was also responsible for notable local public buildings including the clubhouse at Birnam Wood Golf Club and a wing of the Santa Barbara Museum of Art. Built in 1964, the single story, U-shaped abode is sited in the midst of California oaks, its rooms oriented toward the sublime mountain view, with a rectangular swimming pool at its center. It's a stunning example of the primary hallmark of California modernism: bringing the outdoors inside.

The elegant simplicity of the architecture captivated its current owners. Firooz Zahedi is an internationally renowned photographer, and Beth Rudin DeWoody is one of the world's top contemporary art collectors. Devoted aficionados of architecture, this visionary power couple shares residences in New York, West Palm Beach, and Los Angeles; they knew exactly how to update Warner's design. "We enhanced elements

THE CREATIVE COLLECTORS

that gave it more of a Hollywood Regency flavor," says Zahedi. This included changing the color palette of the house to white and gray, and adding contrasting decorative moldings to the interior and exterior doors. But the original footprint of the house remains entirely intact—a testament to the integrity of its modernist design. "The house has a great flow," notes Zahedi. "One room just opens to the other. It's airy, it's bright, it has great walls for art."

In fact, the generous wall space is the primary locus for displaying the couple's unerring talent for visual display. Of course, curating contemporary art in a domestic setting is a balancing act that inevitably incites debate. "We always have this kind of back-and-forth," DeWoody acknowledges, "but at the end of the day, it all comes together." One thing the pair agreed upon from the start was the location of an exquisite mural by legendary California ceramicist Beatrice Wood; as the backdrop for the kitchen's banquette, it is at the center of daily life.

Without a doubt, the most striking space is the living room, a spectacular twelve-foot-high great room with floor-to-ceiling windows on two ends—clearly intended by the architect as a central area for gathering and gazing. One wall is entirely glass, framing a full view of the pristine pool and the Santa Ynez mountains in the distance. Directly opposite, the mirrored fireplace flanked by a luminous site-specific poured-glass wall installation by Rob Wynne, reflects the magnificent mountain view. Two bronze orbs by Lucio Fontana balance on the Lucite coffee table, fronted by a gray sofa and two slipper chairs by renowned designer Chahan Minassian. To the left of the fireplace, a vibrant abstract painting by Louise Fishman hovers over an eye-popping red-orange John McCracken resin sculpture.

The dining room is flooded with light, aided by a glowing Gisela Colón wall sculpture; the dining table displays a collection of whimsical ostrich egg bird sculptures. A trio of paintings—by Gene Davis, Oskar Fischinger, and Claudio Verna—dominates a hallway, seemingly engaged in conversation. The presence of art extends to the outdoors as well, where sculptures by Beverly Pepper and Harry Bertoia mingle in the minimalist garden designed by Zahedi. The entire home, both inside and out, fosters a stimulating dialogue among materials, colors, and imagery—a perfect marriage of art and architecture.

PAGE 158 The great room faces the rectangular pool, framing a sweeping floor-to-ceiling view of the Santa Ynez mountains beyond. Two slipper chairs and a couch, all designed by Chahan Minassian, surround the Lucite coffee table.

PAGES 160–61 This John L. Warner-designed home is a pristine example of California modernism, updated with a white-and-gray color scheme to enhance its Hollywood Regency flavor. The sculpture is by Beverly Pepper.

PAGE 162 A dynamic abstract painting by Louise Fishman commands attention in the great room, fronted by a bright orange John McCracken resin sculpture. In the foreground, Cubo chairs by Jorge Zalszupin face each other across a bronze bowl by Alma Allen.

PAGE 163 The mirrored fireplace in the great room reflects the mountain view and is flanked by a poured-glass installation by Rob Wynne. The Lucite coffee table is graced by two Lucio Fontana bronze orbs.

PAGE 164 The powder room is a dramatic ensemble of black, white, and bronze. The étagerè holds a collection of small sculptures by Claudia DeMonte, Sorel Etrog, and Nancy Lorenz.

PAGE 165 In the hallway, paintings by (left to right) Gene Davis, Oskar Fischinger, and Claudio Verna emphasize the linear geometry of the house.

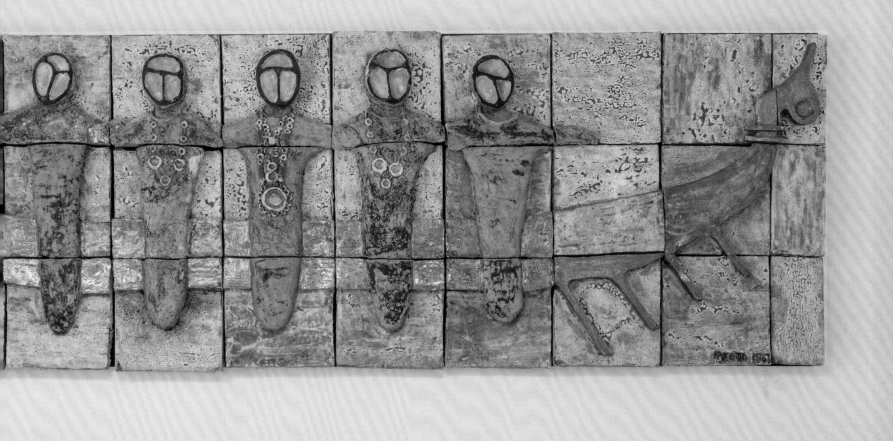

PAGES 166–67 A luminous Gisela Colón wall sculpture provides a glowing backdrop for the glass-topped dining room table, which displays a collection of whimsical ostrich-egg sculptures and candlesticks by Gabriella Crespi.

PAGE 168 The seafoam-green kitchen has a newly tiled wall and terrazzo countertops.

PAGE 169 The breakfast nook displays an exquisite multipanel work by legendary California ceramicist Beatrice Wood.

PAGE 170 A Rashid Johnson ceramic pot and a work on paper by Larry Johnson mingle with colorful furniture in the TV room.

PAGE 171 A portrait of owner Beth DeWoody by Marc Dennis establishes the relaxed air of the TV room, rounded out by a gold lamp by Pedro Friedeberg and another Rashid Johnson ceramic pot.

PAGES 172–73 The owners' poodle, Rooz, lounges in the main bedroom. *IF* by Ed Ruscha hovers near a graphic Piero Fornasetti console, which houses a Sacha Brassoff lamp and bronzes by Gabriella Crespi (left) and Alma Allen (right). The abstract painting over the bed is by Marc Horowitz.

PAGE 174 Decorative moldings were added to the cabinet doors in the main bedroom to play up the home's Hollywood Regency aspects. The bookcase features a blue painting by Forrest Hibbits, a glass foot by Rob Wynne, and a collection of California pottery. In the foreground, a Jean Royère chair fronts an Alexandre Noll sculpture.

PAGE 175 A gilded étagère in the main bedroom displays an eclectic collection of objets, including a white ceramic vessel by Mårten Medbo (top center), a circle piece by Ugo Rondinone (upper right), a John McCracken black resin sculpture (middle right), and two angular vases by Zaha Hadid (below left).

PAGE 176 A bronze sculpture by Harry Bertoia gleams in the afternoon sun next to a mature California live oak.

THIS ICONIC RESIDENCE has a fascinating and charming history that begins with architect George Washington Smith's nontraditional career trajectory. Despite having studied architecture at Harvard University, at the time he designed this home, Smith was actively pursuing a career as a landscape painter (he even made sure the plans for the couple's future abode contained a spacious, double-volume, north-facing space for his art studio). His wife, Mary Smith, purportedly parted with family jewelry to help finance the home's construction. When exchanging her gems for a new home, however, Mrs. Smith likely had no idea her husband would become a standard-bearer of Spanish colonial revival architecture in California.

The 1918 home's simple but majestic Andalusian-inspired design was greeted with such public acclaim (including features in several national architecture publications and glossy magazines) that Smith was persuaded to change professions. Even today, Smith's first residence is frequently cited by historians as a stellar example of his

A CLASSICAL BEGINNING

work, possessing added resonance as the birthplace of his architectural career. In little more than a decade he designed eighty buildings in the Santa Barbara area alone.

For architecture enthusiasts, the first building designed by every notable architect merits examination for clues about the evolution of that architect's work. In this regard, Smith's first home is fascinating, as it truly provides a roadmap of what was to come. The fundamental vocabulary and essential elements of the architect's oeuvre are easily gleaned by viewing the structure: tile floors, wood-beamed ceilings, thick plaster walls, and cement grilles are all present, as is the axial garden with its decorative fountain, which is visually and physically accessed through French doors from both living and dining rooms. These basic yet sophisticated elements derived from Spanish architecture would continue to be combined and refined by Smith over time. But his original artist studio remains sui generis.

The current owner of Smith's first house, who spent her formative years in Montecito, is dedicated to keeping the spirit of this architectural gem alive. The former art studio has morphed into a dramatic, light-flooded living space, filled with jewel-toned fabrics, antiques, and art. The ground-floor living and dining rooms, their original corner fireplaces intact, open gracefully onto the brick terrace. The formal parterre garden overflows with vibrant blooms, and the fountain remains a serene focal point.

PAGE 178 Completed in 1918, this Andalusian-inspired home was designed by George Washington Smith for his own family and provides visual clues about the architect's future creations. It is frequently cited by historians as a stellar example of his work.

PAGES 180-81 This spacious, double-volume space once served as Smith's art studio. The triangular fireplace and thick plastered walls are hallmarks of the architect's home design. The current owner has filled the north-facing room with jewel-toned fabrics, antiques, and art.

PAGE 182 Built-in bookshelves are hidden behind original crimson wood doors in Smith's former painting studio.

PAGE 183 Touchstones of Smith's design—here, in the dining room—include tile floors, wood-beamed ceilings, and another distinctive triangular fireplace.

PAGE 184 The axial garden, with its decorative fountain, is visually and physically accessed through French doors from both living and dining rooms.

A TOWER OF BATTERED VINTAGE FRENCH SUITCASES stands just inside the front door of Kristine and Shane Brown's home. This totem of travel is an apt emblem, as the two spend much of their time scouring the world for unique items to stock their antique emporiums. These include The Well, located in nearby Summerland, and Big Daddy's in Los Angeles, a favorite source for interior designers and celebrity homeowners. Not surprisingly, the Brown residence is a treasure trove of interesting objects.

Recent transplants to Montecito, the Browns acquired their ranch-style home, designed by Paul E. Unander and built in 1958, in 2018. From the start, the home's architecture was almost beside the point. Having spent over three decades creating vignettes of furniture, found objects, and flora for sale, Shane instantly knew the display cabinet he discovered in Belgium years earlier would work perfectly as a space divider in the living room. Kristine's focus was the back yard, where

WILD AND WHIMSICAL

there was ample room for their animal menagerie, including several alpacas, chickens, three dogs, and a goose. With the planned addition of a swimming pool for their two daughters, it was the perfect fit.

Given their expertise, decorating the home was an intuitive process. Indeed, one has the impression that everything in the house has been there forever. As Kristine says of her husband, "Spatially, he's like a savant." Shane honed his keen eye and talent for spotting desirable collectibles during childhood trips with his grandfather to flea markets; an early visit to Hearst Castle with his grandmother helped instill his understanding of monumental scale and the visual power of antiques.

A right turn at the suitcase stack leads to the kitchen, where the back wall is peppered with old cutting boards of all shapes and sizes. Nearby, a colorful work by American modernist painter Stuart Davis presides over a collection of cast iron dogs from England, France, and the United States, scattered on the metal-clad fireplace under a mantel stocked with vellum books. In the hallway's metal display cabinet, two nineteenth-century French bulldog "growler" toys made of papier-mâché share space with silver loving cups and antique vellum books from the fifteenth to eighteenth centuries. The dining room's expansive French monastery table dates from the seventeenth century and is covered with a collection of antique pottery, some recovered from old shipwrecks. A gaggle of vintage dog portraits hovers over the well-worn leather couch in the living room, a spot frequented by the family's three canines. The serene tone-on-tone main bedroom has custom-made windows opening onto the back yard, a headboard fashioned from a French wine-tasting table, and a Swedish dresser topped with treasured collectibles.

The eclectic décor continues outdoors, where a custom-designed Big Daddy's pergola is illuminated by a light fixture that was formerly a French bee skep. The pool, surrounded by vintage outdoor furniture, has a direct view of Montecito Peak. "It's a very lived-in house, and a very comfortable house," Kristine says. "We know that not too many people have a house goose."

PAGE 186   In the garden, a custom pergola shades the outdoor dining area, and a French bee skep has been repurposed as a rustic overhead lamp.

PAGE 188   A tower of battered vintage French suitcases stands just inside the front door of Kristine and Shane Brown's home. This totem of travel is an apt emblem, as the two spend much of their time abroad, scouting for unique items to stock their antique emporiums.

PAGE 189   A colorful painting by American modernist Stuart Davis presides over a collection of cast-iron dogs in front of the metal-clad fireplace in the living room.

PAGE 190 Stocked with eclectic items, including two nineteenth-century French bulldog "growler" toys made of papier-mâché, a metal display cabinet Shane discovered in Belgium works as a space divider in the living room.

PAGE 191 The family pets pose under vintage dog portraits.

PAGE 192 In the kitchen, the back wall displays old cutting boards of all shapes and sizes.

PAGE 193 The property has a vegetable garden and a tiny stone garden shed. The family's menagerie includes a goose.

PAGE 194 Vintage furniture surrounds the serene pool and outdoor fireplace, and Montecito Peak overlooks the scene from a distance.

THIS IMPECCABLE COTTAGE-STYLE HOME, with its dormer windows, slate roof, and circular tower, takes its design cues from sixteenth-century Norman architecture and is an outstanding example of the "period" architecture that flourished in Montecito and Santa Barbara during the 1920s and 1930s. Built in 1925, this is the only known Montecito residence designed by Pierpont Davis, an extremely successful Los Angeles–based architect known for his stylish period buildings, including the famous Villa d'Este courtyard apartments in Hollywood. (He also worked on the design for the Pentagon.) Surprisingly, Davis was also an Olympic champion, having garnered a gold medal in sailing at the 1932 Olympics in Los Angeles.

The owner of this exquisite residence, a devoted Francophile, acquired the property twenty years ago knowing it needed refreshing. That the home had never been structurally altered was an important consideration—and a quality the owner felt deserved respect. In keeping with this ethos, the owner limited changes to the building's existing elements. The original kitchen cabinets were retained and served as a design template for additional cabinets. The original floors remain intact, and no interior walls were moved.

A COZY COTTAGE

Frequent buying trips to Paris and its famous Saint Ouen flea market have added a distinct French flavor to the residence, aided by traditional trompe l'œil finishes and inscriptions hand painted by muralist and decorative artist Vidya Gauci. The owner's lovely collection of blue-and-white china is displayed throughout, and toile fabrics in the bedroom also reflect the blue-and-white theme. A baby grand piano holds pride of place in the living room, where the owner has been known to organize concerts featuring students from Santa Barbara's renowned Music Academy of the West. (In a charming coincidence, it seems the home's original owners were also Music Academy patrons.)

Outside, the original parterre garden—with its boxwood borders encircling the fountain—provides a relaxing focal point, and wisteria climbs over a romantic trellis on the east side of the house. A small grove of orange trees is tucked to the side, their blossoms' fragrance mingling with the thriving French lavender plants. Flowers are abundant—a testament to the owner's long and faithful involvement in the Garden Club of Santa Barbara.

On the books: *BEAUTIFUL* MARK D. SIKES, *VERSAILLES A Private Invitation*, *The Most Beautiful Country Towns of Provence*

PAGE 196 This impeccable cottage-style home is an outstanding example of "period" architecture that flourished in Montecito and Santa Barbara during the 1920s and 1930s.

PAGES 198–99 With its dormer windows, slate roof, and circular tower, the home takes its design cues from sixteenth-century Norman architecture. Built in 1925, it is the only Montecito residence known to have been designed by Pierpont Davis, an extremely successful Los Angeles–based architect renowned for his stylish period buildings.

PAGES 200–201 A baby grand piano holds pride of place in the living room, where the owner has been known to organize concerts featuring students from Santa Barbara's Music Academy of the West. Frequent buying trips to Paris and its famous Saint-Ouen flea market have added a distinct French flavor to the residence.

PAGE 202 The owner's lovely collection of blue-and-white china is displayed in the breakfast nook, where the family pet poses on a matching blue-and-white dog cushion.

PAGE 203 While refreshing the home, the owner retained the existing kitchen cabinets and used them as a design template for additional cabinets. The original floors remain intact, and no interior walls were moved.

PAGE 204 The owner's affection for French-inspired furnishings is apparent in the serene main bedroom.

PAGE 205 The original parterre garden—with its boxwood borders encircling a fountain—provides a relaxing focal point for contemplation.

PAGE 206 Wisteria clambers over a romantic trellis on the east side of the house.

C ALIFORNIA LIVE OAK TREES often serve as natural sculptures in residential Montecito landscapes. By day, they provide shelter and shade; at night, they bring a magical ambiance to outdoor landscapes, especially when dramatically lit from below or illuminated by lanterns. Perfectly sited in a grove of oaks, this delightful residence takes full advantage of their quiet beauty.

Originally constructed in the 1990s, the home has been lovingly remodeled by the owner to feel as if "it sprung up in the 1940s." To achieve this effect, salvaged steel windows were used as partitions in the kitchen, while also creating a completely glass-enclosed dining room that projects into the garden. This enchanting space—flanked on one side by a quartet of olive trees and on the other by an outdoor fireplace—embodies Montecito's indoor-outdoor lifestyle.

By design, the floorplan of the house encourages a circular flow of movement from inside to outside. Small details, like the fireplace screens, are identical both inside and out, ensuring that, as the owner says, "everything feels integrated." The interior color scheme is serenely muted, presenting a striking contrast to the vibrant blooms often displayed in the owner's classical pottery collection. The bedroom, with its majestic curtain-enclosed bed, is an oasis of calm, as is the dressing area leading to the glass-enclosed

SERENE RETREAT

bathroom, whose reflective ceiling provides an illusion of extra height—an optical trick the owner gleaned while living in New York City.

Outside, three fountains ensure the sound of bubbling water is ever-present, and a combination of gravel and fan-shaped cobblestones surrounds the colonnaded swimming pool. Derrik Eichelberger of Arcadia Studio Landscape Architecture turned the owner's desire to have the garden "come right to the house" into a beautiful reality. "When you're here," the owner reflects, "you really feel like you're in the center of the world."

DISFARMER The Vintage Prints

CHRISTIAN SIRIANO

PAGE 208 Nestled in a grove of California live oak trees, this delightful residence, constructed in the 1990s, was lovingly remodeled by the owner to feel as if "it sprung up in the 1940s."

PAGE 210 Salvaged steel windows were used to create a completely glass-enclosed dining room that projects into the garden, an enchanting space flanked on one side by olive trees and on the other by an outdoor fireplace.

PAGE 211 The interior color scheme is serenely muted, presenting a striking contrast to the vibrant blooms displayed in the owner's classical pottery collection.

PAGES 212–13 By design, the home's floorplan encourages movement from inside to outside. A quartet of olive trees is on an axis with the rectangular pool, which is fronted by a square fountain.

PAGES 214–15 The living room's decorative fireplace screen has a twin that adorns the outdoor fireplace, ensuring that, as the owner says, "everything feels integrated." A collection of art and objects is displayed on the glass-topped industrial-style table.

PAGE 216 An arched cabinet in the kitchen provides storage for the owner's extensive collection of tableware.

PAGE 217 The black-and-white kitchen has an intimate scale, and the expansive marble backsplash provides a perfect backdrop for displaying cooking implements and culinary delights.

PAGE 218 The bedroom, with its majestic curtain-enclosed bed, is an oasis of calm.

PAGE 219 The dressing area leads to a glass-enclosed bathroom. The reflective ceiling provides an illusion of extra height—an optical trick the owner gleaned while living in New York City.

PAGE 220 The garden offers a sweeping mountain view above the colonnaded swimming pool.

F EW SPOTS IN MONTECITO can rival the sheer density of lush landscape that surrounds this monumental residence. Its exotic greenery can be traced to the early 1900s, when landscape architect Charles Frederick Eaton—an insatiable collector of plants from around the world—designed several gardens in the area, including his own. Eaton's land was acquired by members of Chicago's meatpacking Armour family to complete their seventy-acre estate, known as El Mirador. Extensively enhanced throughout the 1920s by landscape designer Elmer M. Awl, the immense property ultimately included Italian and Japanese gardens, an outdoor theater, and a private zoo.

Like many grand estates, El Mirador was eventually subdivided into five separate parcels, one of which became the home for this stately Mediterranean-style mansion. Created in the 1990s by local designer Mark DeRose, who also designed its formal gardens, the residence was previously owned by legendary art dealer Stephen Hahn, benefactor of the eponymous Hahn Hall at Santa Barbara's Music Academy of the West.

The home's stunning setting and historic provenance captivated current owner Jeff Abrams as he followed the tree-lined driveway to the home's palatial entrance on his first visit in 2018. "Once the house was revealed to me," he says, "I had this emotional, visceral reaction to it. It reminded me of being in Europe." Such memories are an important touchstone for Abrams, a fashion entrepreneur whose company, Rails, owes its name to his post-college Eurail travel adventures.

Since acquiring the property, Abrams has taken a thoughtful approach to the interior's décor. "My plan is to go a little bit slowly and make sure the pieces I'm bringing in feel like they have a purpose—but also an emotional meaning," he says. "I'm in no rush to make sure that every room is a hundred percent finished"—a reasonable course of action given the mansion's heroic, nearly twelve-thousand-square-foot dimensions. Fortunately, Abrams retained the exquisite four-

DISCREET GRANDEUR

poster metal bed frame commissioned decades earlier by Stephen Hahn for the main bedroom, its pointed finials mirroring the room's arched windows.

Confident in his own taste and encouraged by talented local interior designer Elizabeth Vallino, Abrams journeyed to France to find the appropriate shade of French limestone for the spacious ground floor. On subsequent European trips, he acquired several notable artworks: a colorful nineteenth-century Italian narrative painting presides over the fireplace in the living room; a regal seventeenth-century landscape by Dutch painter Dirk Maas holds court in the library; and the guest bedroom is adorned by two eighteenth-century Venetian landscape paintings. An old adobe from the original Armour estate remains on the property and has been carefully restored as a guest house. The structure is thoughtfully decorated with vintage finds, and its original textured walls and fireplace remain intact.

With an eye to the future, Abrams has acquired an adjacent parcel, also formerly part of the Armour estate, which includes the estate's original gatehouse, the original Japanese garden, and a stone grotto. "I am currently working to create a cohesive landscape story that reflects the original intention of the property," he says.

PAGE 222 A verdant landscape surrounds this monumental residence, sited on land that was once part of a grand estate established in the early 1900s. Built in the 1990s and designed by Mark DeRose, the mansion's stunning setting and historic provenance captivated current owner Jeff Abrams. "It reminded me of being in Europe," he says.

PAGE 224 The mansion's grand entry features a swirling staircase with an intricate wrought-iron balustrade.

PAGE 225 Abrams has taken a thoughtful approach to the interior's décor. "My plan is to go a little bit slowly and make sure the pieces I'm bringing in feel like they have a purpose—but also an emotional meaning," he says. A colorful nineteenth-century Italian narrative painting presides over the fireplace in the living room.

PAGE 226 The guest house—an old adobe from the original estate—has been carefully restored. A vintage leather chair fronts a built-in cabinet containing a collection of colorful textiles.

PAGE 227 The textured walls and fireplace of the adobe remain intact, and the interior has been thoughtfully decorated with vintage finds.

PAGE 228 In the main bedroom, Abrams retained the exquisite four-poster metal bed frame commissioned decades earlier by Stephen Hahn. Its pointed finials mirror the room's arched windows.

PAGE 229 In a guest room, an eighteenth-century painting (one of a pair Abrams acquired in Italy), flanks the bedside.

PAGE 230 The nearly twelve-thousand-square-foot residence features many custom details, including this wrought-iron grille combined with an electric candle sconce.

PAGE 231 The old adobe faces a tennis court.

PAGE 232 A reflection pool with a classical fountain is surrounded by tall palm trees. Mark DeRose created the estate's formal gardens, and some of the exotic greenery can be traced to the early 1900s, when landscape architect Charles Frederick Eaton designed several gardens in the area.

"I THINK YOU BROUGHT BACK EVERYTHING BUT THE CHÂTEAU!" a visitor teased after viewing this enchanting, antiques-filled retreat, which palpably celebrates a lifelong affinity for all things French. Its chatelaine, Renée Parker-Werner, along with her late husband, Gordon, also kept a pied-à-terre in Paris's sixteenth arrondissement, the decorative source for their Montecito mise-en-scène. Clearly this peripatetic couple was fearless when it came to importing large items—including a nineteenth-century wrought-iron gate and an entire room of elaborate *boiserie*—from Europe to their California home. Perhaps Parker-Werner's decades-long stint as a flight attendant is responsible for her charming nonchalance, as she points to a particular object and says, "So that came across the ocean, too…"

It is a magical setting where one feels transported to another place and time. The kitchen, with its colorful array of enamel pots and pans and vintage glassware, looks familiar, as if it might have been depicted elsewhere in a still-life painting. The gnarled trunk of an ancient trumpet vine slouches like a silent visitor against the main doorway, its branches slowly snaking their way outside through the roof. The intricately paneled living room, filled with

ENCHANTING HIDEAWAY

shelves of old books, boasts a beloved baby grand, and its comfy, well-worn leather furniture invites lounging and daydreaming. The tall windows are framed by balloon valances of rosy silk damask that gently filter and tint the incoming light. The bedroom, dominated by a dramatically veiled headboard above the bed, faces a tiny, light-filled sunroom consisting entirely of salvaged antique windows. The atmosphere is Old World; everything is perfect in its imperfection.

Dating from 1911, the structure was originally built as the stable for a grand estate that now exists only in memory. Parker-Werner, who is also a self-taught landscape designer, was introduced to the property twenty-five years ago when she was hired to design its garden by the man who ultimately became her husband. Thereafter, the initial garden assignment expanded to the entire residence, a project she has been passionately focused on for more than a decade.

Of course, the outdoor surroundings are every bit as stunning as the home's interiors, with copious groupings of rose bushes and an expansive wisteria arbor that serves as a plein-air dining room. There's even a small, carefully tended orchard that yields lemons, oranges, and avocados. Naturally, Parker-Werner makes good use of her "shed," a tiny haven packed with well-used flower-arranging tools and her collection of antique French gardening implements, artfully displayed above the corner fireplace.

PAGE 234 Just inside the main doorway of this tiny home, the gnarled trunk of an ancient trumpet vine slouches like a silent visitor, its branches snaking their way outside through the roof.

PAGES 236–37 Dating from 1911, the structure was originally built as the stable for a grand estate that now exists only in memory. Renée Parker-Werner, a self-taught landscape designer, was introduced to the property twenty-five years ago when she was hired to design its garden by the man who ultimately became her husband. She has been working on it ever since, and the results are sublime.

PAGES 238–39 Parker-Werner's coveted "shed" is a haven packed with well-used flower-arranging tools and a collection of antique French gardening implements, artfully displayed above the corner fireplace.

PAGES 240–41 The kitchen, with its colorful enamelware and vintage glassware, looks familiar, as if it might have been depicted in a still-life painting.

PAGES 242–43 The antiques-filled retreat, which celebrates a lifelong affinity for all things French, is a magical setting where one feels transported to another place and time. An eclectic gathering of vintage baskets, pottery, and unframed paintings surrounds a white brick fireplace in one of the home's cozy rooms.

PAGE 244 A light-filled sunroom is composed entirely of antique salvaged windows.

I F A TRUE TEST OF ANY ARCHITECT'S TALENT is how long their buildings remain relevant, then this repurposed residence exemplifies the enduring genius of George Washington Smith. Built in 1928, this structure was designed as a combination garage and gardener's cottage to service a twenty-seven-acre estate known as Quien Sabe. Owned by New York native John D. Wright and his wife, Isabel, the estate was landscaped with exotic plants. But within a decade the Wrights had moved back to New York, Smith's plans for the estate's grand manor house were never realized, and Quien Sabe was ultimately subdivided into several parcels.

In the 1950s the garage–gardener's cottage was sold to two well-known blacklisted screenwriters, Marguerite Roberts and her husband, John B. Sanford, who sought refuge from Hollywood in Montecito. (The couple was truly talented: Roberts scripted the John Wayne film *True Grit*, and Sanford's five-volume autobiography won a PEN/Faulkner Award.) They remodeled the garage and transformed the entire building into a living space,

HARMONIC RESONANCE

remaining there until the end of their lives. The property subsequently changed hands several times, improved by the addition of a pool and guest quarters, all in harmony with Smith's style.

The current owner is intimately familiar with Smith's architecture, having previously owned a mansion designed in 1920 by the architect. The consistency of Smith's aesthetic is such that much of the contents of the owner's prior residence have seamlessly translated to this one. Indeed, the home's proportions, including the generous archways and high ceilings, seem ready-made for the owner's possessions. Specifically chosen to emphasize the Moorish characteristics of the architect's oeuvre, the furnishings include antiques gathered on trips to Morocco and Paris, combined with the family's collection of nineteenth-century jewel-toned paintings. Antique walnut Syrian throne chairs inlaid with mother-of-pearl surround the dining room table, and an array of blue-and-white pottery and ancient tiles are displayed in nearby niches. An elaborate mirrored console table by Carlo Bugatti graces the entryway. Nearly every room possesses an exotic textile from the owner's carefully curated collection. A wrought-iron balustrade lines the tile-clad stairs leading to the second level, where a serene private loggia overlooks the garden toward the ocean beyond.

The garden itself features descendants of the exotic plants that were part of the landscape at Quien Sabe, including the spiny cacti the owner has assembled like sentries near the front entrance. A bubbling fountain is the backdrop for the parterre garden, visible from the living room through the arched doorways of the building's former garage doors.

George Washington Smith's simple garage and gardener's cottage, having been happily inhabited for nearly a century, clearly receive the same level of attention and thought as his grand creations—and the results are ultimately just as iconic.

PAGE 246 A lovely example of Spanish Colonial Revival, this building was originally designed by George Washington Smith as a combination garage and gardener's cottage for a large—but never completed—estate known as Quien Sabe. The garage portion was transformed into living space in the 1950s, and the garden features descendants of the exotic plants that were part of Quien Sabe's landscape, including the spiny cacti stationed like sentries near the front entrance.

PAGES 248–49 The pool and guest quarters are recent additions, but both are in harmony with Smith's distinctive architectural style.

PAGE 250 A bubbling fountain is the backdrop for a parterre garden, visible from the living room through the arched doorways of the building's former garage doors.

PAGE 251 The furnishings and antiques emphasize the Moorish characteristics of Smith's design. Antique walnut Syrian throne chairs inlaid with mother-of-pearl surround the dining room table, and an array of blue-and-white pottery and ancient tiles are displayed in nearby niches.

PAGES 252–53 The seating area adjacent to the kitchen includes inlaid wood occasional tables. Its yellow accents recall the large yellow pottery urns flanking the pool.

PAGE 254 A tiled staircase with an intricate wrought-iron balustrade leads to the second floor.

PAGE 255 The back wall of the kitchen is clad in an exuberant mix of colorful patterned tiles, providing a lively backdrop for the owner's collection of brightly hued pottery.

PAGE 256 The second-floor bathroom is an oasis of calm. The delightful inlaid wood vanity has a pristine marble top, and the stained-glass windows provide filtered light.

PAGE 257 The main bedroom has a small balcony overlooking the garden and pool area. The pastel color scheme is reflected in the gold-framed nineteenth-century painting, part of the family's extensive art collection.

PAGE 258 A bedroom in the guest quarters has a coral-and-gold color scheme and features an elaborate Suzani textile.

PAGE 259 The living room of the guest quarters is decorated with a mix of antique and contemporary objects and art.

PAGES 260–61 The guest quarters open directly onto a blue-tiled rectangular pool that reflects the house and is surrounded by palm trees.

PAGE 262 The second-floor loggia has a series of open archways overlooking the garden.

THERE'S SOMETHING FASCINATING about the homes architects design for themselves. Free from client demands, the spaces seem less restrained, and they are often smaller (likely because of to the lack of client-sized budgets). Lutah Maria Riggs, Santa Barbara's first licensed female architect, was thirty years old in 1926 when she designed her own Andalusian-inspired home, Clavelitos (little carnation), and it is where she resided for almost six decades until her death in 1984.

Sadly, when interior designer Richard Hallberg first walked through the doors of Clavelitos sixteen years ago, the residence and surrounding garden were in serious disrepair. An avid Riggs admirer, Hallberg was undeterred and embraced the opportunity to restore the architect's creation. Clearly a labor of love, the results are sublime. The thick white walls, paneled Dutch doors, wood-beam ceilings, and geometric tile floors are perfectly intact, as is the gracious archway in the living room that frames the steep staircase tethered

CLASSIC REVIVAL

by a simple rope handrail. This last detail can also be seen in the first house designed by Riggs's employer, celebrated architect George Washington Smith. But Riggs, who served as principal designer in Smith's office, ultimately developed a successful solo career, as well as her own singular style.

In Hallberg's talented hands, Riggs's personal vision has come back to life. The designer filled the space with an array of unique objects collected on his travels, as well as items formerly belonging to Riggs, purchased from Montecito antiques dealer Michael Haskell. "I really didn't want to do anything to the house that would change it or make it feel that I was trying to impose anything but what she wanted," Hallberg says. "I tried to get inside her brain." Indeed, the designer was inspired to adapt one of the home's architectural details for one of his own design projects.

The handsome garden colonnade was added by Hallberg in homage to Riggs and Smith, who included similar allées in their garden designs. But credit is clearly due to Hallberg for the inviting outdoor rooms, all of which align with the architecture of the house. His stated intent, to envelop the house in green, was clearly realized. Focal points within the garden include a serene path leading to a stone sculpture of an open book and a charming seventeenth-century stone lion that presides over the pool. The pool itself is surrounded by wonderfully mismatched stones left over from antique fireplaces that were reduced to fit inside twenty-first-century homes.

PAGE 264 Santa Barbara's first female architect, Lutah Maria Riggs, designed this Andalusian-inspired home for herself in 1926. Designer Richard Hallberg acquired the home sixteen years ago and embraced the opportunity to restore the architect's creation. The home's thick white walls, wood-beamed ceilings, and geometric tile floors are perfectly intact, as is the living room's gracious archway that frames a steep staircase tethered by a simple rope handrail.

PAGES 266-67 A moss-covered fountain centered inside a square reflection pond greets visitors in the home's entry courtyard.

PAGES 268-69 The living room displays an eclectic collection of furniture and objects. According to Hallberg, "the house is a conglomeration of things I love. It wasn't really a design project. It was just a labor of love."

PAGE 270 A collection of animal sculptures is gathered on a rustic wood table in the living room.

PAGE 271 Distinctive paneled wood doors cover a small window, and a similar design is repeated in the cabinets below. "I really didn't want to do anything to the house that would change it," Hallberg says. "When I built new cabinets, I built cabinets that were similar to the cabinets that [Riggs] did."

PAGE 272 A metal-framed four-poster bed reaches toward the high wood-beamed ceiling in the bedroom. Dutch doors—original to the building—provide access to the outside.

PAGE 273 The narrow bathroom features a copper-sided bathtub and two rough-hewn stone sinks.

PAGE 274 A collection of green pottery adorns the dining room table. Riggs included Dutch doors as a signature detail throughout the home. "They're practical," notes Hallberg. "They really work well."

PAGE 275 Hallberg filled the home with his favorite items, including a delightful collection of hand brushes.

PAGES 276-77 A small bedroom has its own fireplace and a tiny built-in nook for reading.

PAGES 278-79 Hallberg created several inviting outdoor rooms, all of which align with the architecture of the house. A seventeenth-century stone lion presides over the rectangular pool, which is surrounded by mismatched stones left over from antique fireplaces.

PAGE 280 A secluded spot in the garden is surrounded by leafy hedges.

FOR JANE AND MARC NATHANSON, "home" is where the art is. In each of their three residences—located in Los Angeles, Aspen, and Montecito—examples of their extensive collection of blue-chip postwar and contemporary artwork are on prominent display. "People and art are the color in all of my houses," Jane says. "The main focus is the art, the color is the art, and everything [else] is supposed to be muted and fade into the background."

Even so, the graceful Mediterranean-style architecture of their Montecito residence, acquired in 2021, serves as a powerful foil for the couple's eye-popping collection. Built in 1975, it is one of the last homes designed by architect Wallace Neff, whose career included a stint working for the pioneer of Spanish Colonial Revival architecture, George Washington Smith. Neff subsequently forged a successful career in Pasadena and Los Angeles, designing estates for Hollywood moguls and screen stars. His renown among the entertainment elite endures posthumously: Brad Pitt, Madonna, Barbra Streisand, and Diane Keaton have all owned Neff-designed homes.

The Nathansons placed the task of combining their art collection with Neff's architecture into the creative hands of designer Richard Hallberg. The ceilings and floors were transformed from dark brown to a light gray, the walls were painted brilliant white, and a wrought-iron staircase was plastered in, providing additional wall space for the art. "We just cleaned and modernized it," Hallberg says, "without dishonoring the architecture of the house."

The result is astonishing. Art commands the viewer's eye in every space, while Neff's architectural details—arched windows and doorways—complement the gestural quality of the art. In the high-ceilinged living room, a vibrant three-dimensional painting by Charles Hinman is centered over the stone fireplace. Titled *Always a Larger Context*, this painting has the distinction of being the first piece in the Nathansons' joint collection, a 1966 wedding engagement gift from Jane's parents. A custom table by Fernando Mastrangelo fronts the fireplace, bookended by two custom

ART HOUSE

chaise longues. On the opposite wall, a metal sculpture by Anish Kapoor floats above a custom banquette, creating a silvery presence that reflects light and movement in the room. An enormous slab of rough-hewn selenite crystal serves as a dramatic coffee table, flanked by two wood-frame Geo chairs by Formations. An enormous, deep-pile white rug covers the floor, creating soft peaks and waves around the furniture.

The Minimalist dining room is dominated by Doug Aitken's mirrored sculpture *More* which hovers over a floating white lacquer console. Nearby, Marc Sijan's hyperrealistic security guard sculpture is posted at the window. The sleek white lacquer dining table is surrounded by Paola Lenti's woven chairs. In the family room, Biff Heinrich's photographic print *Pool* invokes a casual atmosphere, and the custom banquette provides a perfect backdrop for the massive triangular coffee table by Ben Storms, which is topped by a whimsical Jeff Koons *Puppy* vase.

Old Couple on a Bench, a signature lifelike sculpture by Duane Hanson, sits outside the downstairs bedroom, which features a graphic red-black-and-white piece by Barbara Kruger and a bright red Pony chair by Eero Aarnio. Upstairs, Mitchell Syrop's exhortative piece *Pull Yourself Together* is suspended over the fireplace in the main bedroom.

As a trained psychologist, Jane firmly believes that art and culture are vital to our well-being as a society, and her Montecito home is an inspiring example. She'll soon have more walls to fill, given Marc's appointment as the US ambassador to Norway. "I hear they have a real burgeoning contemporary art community there," Jane says with a delighted smile, "so I'm looking forward to it."

PAGE 282 This graceful Mediterranean-style home, built in 1975, is one of the last homes designed by architect Wallace Neff, whose career included a stint working for the pioneer of Spanish Colonial Revival architecture, George Washington Smith.

PAGE 284 A metal sculpture by Anish Kapoor floats above a custom banquette in the living room. The dramatic coffee table, an enormous slab of rough-hewn selenite crystal, is flanked by two wood-frame Geo chairs by Formations.

PAGE 285 A vibrant three-dimensional painting by Charles Hinman is centered over the stone fireplace; it has the distinction of being the first piece in the owners' significant art collection. A custom cement-and-crystal table by Fernando Mastrangelo fronts the fireplace, bookended by two custom chaise longues.

PAGES 286–87 The Minimalist dining room is dominated by Doug Aitken's mirrored sculpture *More*, which hovers over a floating white console. Nearby, Marc Sijan's hyperrealistic security guard sculpture is posted at the window. The sleek, white lacquer dining table is surrounded by Paola Lenti's woven chairs.

PAGES 288–89 In the main bedroom, Mitchell Syrop's exhortative piece, *Pull Yourself Together*, is suspended over the fireplace.

PAGE 290 *Old Couple on a Bench*, a signature lifelike sculpture by Duane Hansen, sits outside the downstairs bedroom, which features the graphic red-black-and-white piece *Untitled (Whose?)* by Barbara Kruger and a bright red Pony chair by Eero Aarnio.

PAGE 291 John Baldessari's *Blue Boy* is stationed just outside the yellow-accented guest bedroom.

PAGE 292 In the family room, Biff Heinrich's photograph *Pool* evokes a casual atmosphere, and the custom banquette provides a perfect backdrop for the massive triangular coffee table by Ben Storms, which is topped by a whimsical Jeff Koons *Puppy* vase.

FIROOZ ZAHEDI AND LORIE DEWHIRST PORTER extend heartfelt gratitude to the homeowners who, despite the presence of an ongoing pandemic, graciously opened their doors and permitted us to photograph their extraordinary homes, and enlightened us about the stories behind them. Based on an introduction by Phaidon CEO Keith Fox, our hardworking editor Alan Rapp at Monacelli saw the potential in showcasing an enchanting area that stretches over just a few square miles in Southern California. Our sincere thanks to them both for taking on this project. We are grateful for the insightful foreword generously offered by the renowned architect and California architecture expert Marc Appleton. The responsibility of designing a book that combines both photographs and text is not an easy task; it was our good fortune to have the talented Phil Kovacevich on our team.

Firooz Zahedi thanks Lorie Dewhirst Porter, not only for conveying her knowledge of the architectural history of Montecito in her skilled writing, but also her support in fine-tuning the settings for photography. Thanks to Frank Schaefer, a digital expert, whose assistance made the photographs look as good as they do. Thanks also to my son Darian Zahedi for his assistance, and to my wife Beth Dewoody for her research and constant support. I would also like to

ACKNOWLEDGMENTS

extend my thanks to Jason Streatfeild for finding our Montecito home for us, and to Becker Studios, especially Andy Becker and Jose Sarabia, for their tireless work on our house, as well as Ramon Reyes, a master landscape designer, who brought my vision for our garden to fruition.

Lorie Dewhirst Porter thanks master photographer Firooz Zahedi for kindly giving me the opportunity to collaborate on this book. It has been a truly transformative experience. My wonderful parents, Joan and Robert Dewhirst, provided a creative childhood for me and my sisters, enabling us to start our lives in a midcentury masterpiece by architect Daniel N. Salerno, followed by the hands-on construction of our second home (aided by my Uni High School friends). These environments, both in the hills of Los Angeles, forged my enduring love for architecture. My husband and soulmate, architect Michael Patrick Porter—who designed and literally built, along with my father, the delightful home where we live—inspires me every day.

Library of Congress Control Number: 2022938436

ISBN 978-1-58093-595-1

10 9 8 7 6 5 4 3 2 1

Printed in China

Design by Phil Kovacevich

Monacelli
A Phaidon Company
65 Bleecker Street
New York, New York 10012

www.monacellipress.com